FIRST MATH

COUNTING

By
Joanna Brundle

KidHaven
PUBLISHING

Published in 2018 by
KidHaven Publishing, an Imprint of Greenhaven Publishing, LLC
353 3rd Avenue
Suite 255
New York, NY 10010

Designer: Danielle Jones
Editor: Joanna Brundle

Cataloging-in-Publication Data

Names: Brundle, Joanna.
Title: Counting / Joanna Brundle.
Description: New York : KidHaven Publishing, 2018. | Series: First math | Includes index.
Identifiers: ISBN 9781534521933 (pbk.) | ISBN 9781534521896 (library bound) | ISBN 9781534521810 (6 pack) | ISBN 9781534521858 (ebook)
Subjects: LCSH: Counting–Juvenile literature.
Classification: LCC QA113.B78 2018 | DDC 513.2'1–dc23

Printed in the United States of America

CPSIA compliance information: Batch #BS17KL: For further information contact Greenhaven Publishing LLC, New York, New York at 1-844-317-7404.

Please visit our website, www.greenhavenpublishing.com. For a free color catalog of all our
high-quality books, call toll free 1-844-317-7404 or fax 1-844-317-7405.

PHOTO CREDITS

**Abbreviations: l-left, r-right, b-bottom,
t-top, c-center, m-middle.**

Front cover – Oksana Kuzmina. 3 – Bloomua. 4 – pukach. 5 – gualtiero boffi. 6 – iava777. 7 – photomaster. 8 – Tim UR. 9 – andersphoto. 10 – Chones. 11 – Erik Lam. 12 – Napat. 13 – ARTSILENSE. 14 – Joe Gough. 15l – Samoilova Helen. 15c – GAMARUBA. 15r – sagir. 16 – Erik Lam & Eric Isselee. 17 – bajinda. 18 – Andrey Armyagov. 19 – Vaclav Volrab. 20 – suns07butterfly. 21t/ml – Rob Wilson. 21bl – Dmitry Kalinovsky. 21tc – StockPhotosArt. 21mc – Brian Kinney. 21cb – Nerthuz. 21tr – Tyler Olson. 21rm – Rob Wilson. 21rb – Masekesam. 22 – creativestockexchange. 23tl – nopporn0510. 23bl – Zerbor. 23tml – arka38. 23bml – Muzhik. 23tc/tmr/tr – Lev Kropotov. 23bc – Production Perig. 23bmr – luckypic. 23br – fotomak. 24tl – Timmary. 24tr – Eric Isselee. 24tl – Carolyn Franks. 24br – sspopov. 24cl – denn61. 24tm – Christian Weber. 24bm – Bjorn Heller. 24tcm – Charles Brutlag. 24bcm&tr – Photobac. 24tmr – s_oleg. 24br – remik44992.

Images are courtesy of Shutterstock.com, with thanks to Getty Images, Thinkstock Photo, and iStockphoto.

CONTENTS

Trace the numbers with your finger as you read.

1

1 2 3

one

one
blue
balloon

4   5   6   7   8   9   10

one
enormous
elephant

⑤

2
two

1 2 3

two
chirpy
chicks

two
pink
piglets

3
three

1 2 3

three
green
grapes

4   5   6   7   8   9   10

three
red
ribbons

4

four

1   2   3

four beach balls

4 5 6 7 8 9 10

four cuddly kittens

5
five

1   2   3

five crunchy carrots

4 **5** 6 7 8 9 10

five playful puppies

6
six

six
sizzling
sausages

4   5   **6**   7   8   9   10

six shiny shoes

7

1   2   3

seven

seven
little
lambs

16

seven sweet strawberries

8 eight

1 2 3

eight floating fish

4   5   6   7   **8**   9   10

eight giant
giraffes

9

nine

1 2 3

nine
beautiful
butterflies

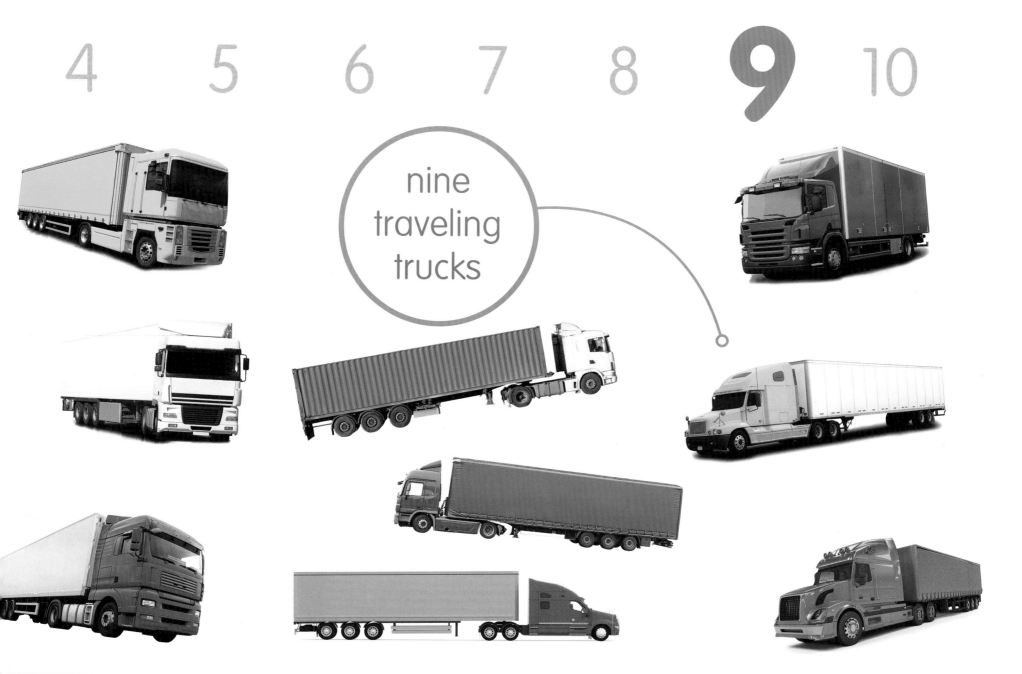

4 5 6 7 8 **9** 10

nine
traveling
trucks

10
ten

ten
colorful
crayons

1   2   3

4 5 6 7 8 9 **10**

ten tall
trees

How Many Can You See?

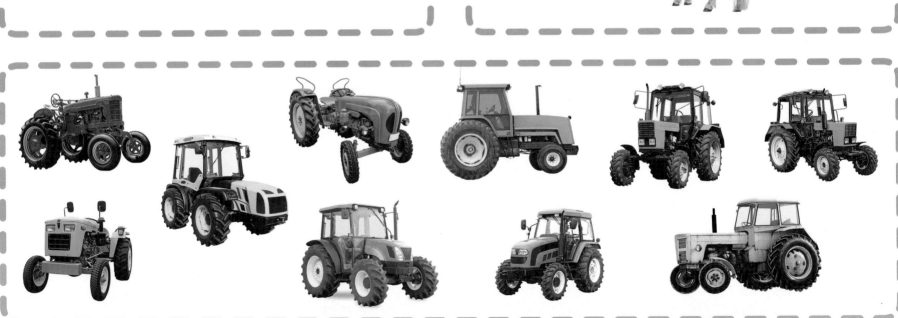

Answers: 3 presents, 6 horses, 10 tractors